HISTORY IS NOT THE PAST.
IT IS THE PRESENT.
WE CARRY OUR HISTORY
WITH US.
WE ARE OUR HISTORY.
—JAMES BALDWIN

* * *

More to Explore

Want to know more about the people, places, and ideas in this book? Start here:

BOOKS

Alexander, Kwame. *The Undefeated.* New York: Versify, 2019.

Bridges, Ruby. *Through My Eyes.* New York: Scholastic Inc., 1999.

Hamilton, Virginia. *Her Stories: African American Folktales, Fairy Tales, and True Tales.* New York: Scholastic Inc., 1995.

Harrison, Vashti. *Little Leaders: Bold Women in Black History.* New York: Little, Brown and Company, 2017.

Harrison, Vashti. Little Legends: *Exceptional Men in Black History.* New York: Little, Brown and Company, 2019.

Hill, Laban Carrick. *Harlem Stomp! A Cultural History of the Harlem Renaissance.* New York: Little, Brown and Company, 2004.

Nelson, Kadir. *We Are the Ship: The Story of Negro League Baseball.* New York: Little, Brown and Company, 2008.

Smith, Charles R., Jr. *28 Days: Moments in Black History that Changed the World.* New York: Roaring Brook Press, 2015.

WEBSITES

African American Registry: https://aaregistry.org

The HistoryMakers: https://www.thehistorymakers.org

The Martin Luther King, Jr. Research and Education Institute: kinginstitute.stanford.edu

Schomburg Center for Research in Black Culture: https://www.nypl.org/locations/schomburg

MUSEUMS

The DuSable Museum of African American History: https://www.dusablemuseum.org

The Equal Justice Initiative: https://www.eji.org

Museum of the African Diaspora: https://www.moadsf.org

National Museum of African American History and Culture: https://nmaahc.si.edu

The Studio Museum in Harlem: https://studiomuseum.org

POETRY

"Booker T. and W. E. B." by Dudley Randall

"Harlem" by Langston Hughes

"Harriet Tubman" by Eloise Greenfield

"Lift Ev'ry Voice and Sing" by James Weldon Johnson

"We Real Cool" by Gwendolyn Brooks

For Santi Sunflower, and the infinite Black imagination. —R.C.

For my mother. —L.S.

Text copyright © 2020 by Rio Cortez

Illustrations copyright © 2020 by Lauren Semmer

Library of Congress Cataloging-in-Publication Data is available.

ISBN 978-1-5235-0749-8

Cover and jacket art by Lauren Semmer

Workman books are available at special discounts when purchased in bulk for premiums and sales promotions as well as for fund-raising or educational use. Special editions or book excerpts can also be created to specification. For details, contact the Special Sales Director at the address below or send an email to special markets@workman.com.

Workman Publishing Co., Inc.
225 Varick Street, New York, NY 10014-4381
workman.com

WORKMAN is a registered trademark of Workman Publishing Co., Inc.

Printed in China
First printing November 2020

10 9 8 7 6 5 4 3 2 1

THE ABCs OF BLACK HISTORY

Words by RIO CORTEZ

Pictures by LAUREN SEMMER

WORKMAN PUBLISHING
NEW YORK

LET US 'TIL VICTORY

A is for **anthem,** a banner of song
   that wraps us in hope, lets us know we belong.
We lift up our voices, lift them and sing.
From stages and street corners, let freedom ring.

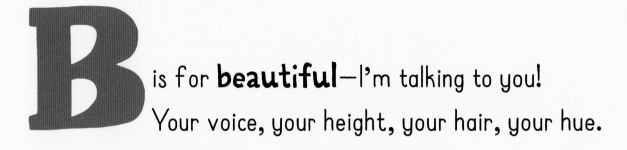

B is for **beautiful**—I'm talking to you!
Your voice, your height, your hair, your hue.

B is for **brave**, for **bright**, and for **bold**.
For those who STOOD UP—even when they were told
to step back, stand down, remember their place.

B is for **brotherhood**, for **believing** in grace.

C is for **community**, where we live, laugh, and eat,
and for **church**, where we worship, mourn, sing, and meet.
Did you hear Reverend King preach on his dream
of **civil** rights, human rights, a powerful theme?

VOTE

CHICAGO

DETROIT

NEW YORK CITY
NAACP

FREEDOM NOW CORE

NORTH
AMERICA

LOS ANGELES

ATLANTA

NEW ORLEANS

MIAMI

ATLANTIC
OCEAN

PACIFIC
OCEAN

CARIBBEAN

N
W E
S

SOUTH
AMERICA

BRAZIL

EURASIA

AFRICA

MALI

SUDAN

INDIAN OCEAN

D is for **diaspora**—pulled from our homes,
we were carried away in ships on the foam
to Haiti, Cuba, America, Brazil.
Our names are different, new, but still:
We are connected. Then, now, forevermore,
to that long ago, faraway African shore.

E is for **explore**—to study a place:
like Matthew Henson, the Arctic;
Mae Jemison, space.

NORTH
90°N
POLE

1 2 3 4 5 6

E is for **education**, for **expanding** the mind,
like Ruby Bridges, Linda Brown, the Little Rock Nine—
The first Black children in all-white schools,
they opened the doors and challenged the rules.

$2 \times 5 = 10$

SCHOOL

ABC

KNOWLEDGE

cat see ru
and d

F is for **food**, grown and **farmed** with our hands, worked and tilled and pulled from the land.

For **fried fish**, ham hocks, warm buttermilk bread,
or maybe the sharp taste of mustards instead.

F is for **folklore** by the light of the moon,
for **family**, for **freedom**, for jumping the broom.

G is for **GO!** Toward cities we were bound.
For the **Great Migration** from country to town.
From farming the land to the factory floor,
we carried the Blues on our backs, not much more.

H is for **Harlem**—those big city streets!
We walked and we danced to our own jazzy beat.
When Louis and Bessie and Duke owned the stage,
and Langston and Zora Neale **Hurston**, the page.

I

is for **imagine, invent, innovative!**
For all of the ways we are so creative!

alvin ailey

jean-michel basquiat

gwendolyn brooks

madam c.j. walker

george Washington carver

dJ Kool herc

J is for **Juneteenth!** We were finally free!
(Or so we hoped in this moment of glee.)

J is for **J'ouvert,** when the drummers drum-drum,
from Trinidad, Grenada, and Haiti they come!

K is for **kin,** our fathers and mothers,
our ancestors, elders, our sisters and brothers.
K is for **Kwanzaa,** which honors that bond.
Ask *Habari gani?* and we might respond:

Umoja (unity) • **Kujichagulia** (self-determination, or believing in your own strength) • **Ujima** (collective work and responsibility, or taking care of our kin) • **Ujamaa** (cooperative economics, or working hard to create new businesses and support other businesses in the community) • **Nia** (purpose) • **Kuumba** (creativity) • **Imani** (faith)

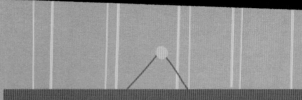

MARSHA P. JOHNSON

ASHLEY & ROSE

OSSIE & RUBY

THE LOVING FAMILY

L is for **love**. L is for **love**. L is always for **love**.

NAT LOVE

M

is for **march**, for lifting our feet,
taking the **movement**, the cause to the street.

Black lives **matter**. Every breath, every dream—
Every thought, each idea, each impossible scheme.

The **might** of our **message** is easy to hear:
The drumbeat of hope is louder than fear.

N is for **newspapers**—we started our own
to tell our stories and let it be known
we deserved the front page! We deserved to be seen!
And to also be featured in slick magazines.

LAUNDROMAT

WE WASH
WHITE
ONLY

OPEN 24HR

OPEN

COLORED
STAYOUT

O is for **organize**, for getting together
to sit-in and boycott to make our lives better.
Thank you, Fred Hampton, thank you, Diane Nash,
for not being afraid of the possible clash
with police, and people who shouted and teased.
Because of you, we can go where we please.

P is for **power.** It's part of our core.
Sometimes it is quiet, sometimes it must ROAR
like a **Panther**—isn't that right, Huey **P.**?
Power for **people** like you and like me.

And who do you think has more **power** than most?
The **president!** Obama was first to that post.
But Shirley Chisholm—unbossed and unbought—
came so much closer than most people thought
a Black woman could, which just goes to show,
P is for **possible,** so glow on, child, glow.

QUEEN AMINA

QUEEN NANDI

TONI MORRISON

Q is for **Queens!**
Behold and bow down!

ANGELA DAVIS

RUBY HURLEY

Maame Biney

ALTHEA GIBSON

USA

R is for **rise**, to **reach** for the top,
relentlessly striving, **refusing** to stop.
Like ballplayers, boxers, and gymnasts who fly,
sprinters and skaters who zoomed right on by
old **records**, old thinking—a sight to behold!
They went for the win and grabbed for the gold.

GABBY DOUGLAS

S is for **scientists** who charted the **stars**, **studied** the bees, took care of our hearts. For Benjamin Banneker, Patricia Bath, for Katherine Johnson's beautiful math.

S is for **soul**—how **sweet** the **sound!**
From the croon of Sam Cooke to the wail of James Brown.
Brother Ray on the keys, Sister Tharpe dressed in mink,
and Queen Aretha **sang,** "You betta think!"

T is for **Tuskegee**, an all-Black school
where students learned **trades** and **toiled** with **tools**.
"That's how we will rise," said boss Booker **T**.
But another smart man just didn't agree.

W. E. B. Du Bois said, "Industry's fine,
but I think it's better to work on your mind."
They had different ideas, but here is what's **true**:
In their own ways, they were thinking of you.

HISTORY

SCIENCE

π MATHEMATICS +

LITERATURE

U is for **United States**—this story is tough.
The birth of a nation was deadly for us.
We the people? In the land of the free?
No one who was enslaved would agree.

U is for **unbroken**, **unshaken**, **unbound**,
like Harriet Tubman, who went **underground**,
took back her freedom and freed *hundreds* more,
then was a spy in the great
Civil War.

But when the states
were united again,
the fight for our freedom
and lives didn't end.
So **U** is for **unfinished**, this American tale.
With courage and strength, we will prevail!

V is for **vote**—do you know what that means?
The freedom to pick and choose as you please.

BLACK
LIVES
MATTER

The freedom to choose who makes the rules,
who has the power, who gets the tools
to make their lives better. That's why we fight.
The freedom to vote is a true civil right!

W is for **writers**, whose **wisdom** and **words**
bring to life **worlds** where our voices are heard.

Rappers and poets and songwriters, too,
all those who spin from our point of view.

BORN
MALCOLM
LITTLE
1925 OMAHA,
NEBRASKA

NEW YORK RED
1940s ROXBURY, BOSTON

PRISONER 22843
1946
CHARLESTON STATE
PRISON

X is for Malcolm, Malik El-Shabazz,
known also as Red, Malcolm Little, El-Hajj.
By any means necessary, he insisted on change,
starting with **X**—he reclaimed his name.

Y is for **young**, gifted
and Black
like Lady Lorraine,
who never looked back.
She wrote of big dreams
in rooms so small
it's hard to believe
they were dreamed in at all.

Lorraine and her work
moved Nina Simone
so much that Nina made
work of her own:
"Young, Gifted and Black,"
a banner of song
that wraps us in hope,
lets us know we belong.

Z is for **zenith**, the highest, the peak!

The top of that mountain King said we would reach.

He won't get there with us, but still we march on,

rising, rising, like the sun with the dawn.

The ABCs of Black History: Terms and Figures

Black history is a story of heartbreak and triumph. Of incredible creativity, joy, and light, sometimes in the face of terrible pain. It is the story of always moving forward, of hope that each day will be better than the one before. Such a story—that spans continents and centuries—is too big to capture here, but we've offered a glimpse. As you read, what connections can you make?

James Baldwin (1924–1987)

James Baldwin was brilliant. He was a child preacher, a novelist, poet, philosopher, and a son of Harlem who thought Black people should be included in America's promise of liberty and justice for all. And he was a gay man who believed that when it comes to love, you should "go the way your blood beats."

A is for Anthem

An anthem is a song that brings people together and gives them a sense of pride. **"Lift Ev'ry Voice and Sing"** was written at a time when Black people were no longer enslaved, but still were not free. Their rights were severely limited, and their lives were threatened every day, especially in the South. They needed something to make them feel strong and to give them hope. "Lift Ev'ry Voice and Sing" is a poem written in the late 1890s by activist and scholar **James Weldon Johnson (1871–1938)** and set to music by his brother, **John Rosamond Johnson (1873–1954)**. In 1919, "Lift Ev'ry Voice and Sing" became the official song of the **National Association for the Advancement of Colored People (NAACP)**—an organization that strives to make life better for Black people—and is unofficially known as the Black national anthem.

B is for Beautiful

We're not the first to say "Black is beautiful." Back in the 1960s and 1970s, Black people were loud and proud about their look, sound, and style. Photographers **Gordon Parks**

(1912–2006) and **Kwame Brathwaite (1938–)** captured that look on film, and *Soul Train,* a music and dance show created by **Don Cornelius (1936–2012)**, celebrated Black style on television.

C is for Community

A community is any group of people that makes you feel welcome. It might be a neighborhood, a school, a mosque, a synagogue, or a church. The church has a special place in Black history. It was a place where African-Americans felt safe and comfortable. In the 1950s, as Black people continued to fight to be fully recognized as human beings, church leaders came together to do their part. They chose **Reverend Martin Luther King, Jr. (1929–1968)**, a young minister at **Dexter Avenue Baptist Church** in Montgomery, Alabama, as their spokesperson. Reverend King went on to become a powerful voice in the fight for civil rights.

D is for Diaspora

African Diaspora refers to the spread of people from the continent of Africa to other parts of the world. From the 1500s to the 1800s, this spread happened because of the transatlantic (across the Atlantic Ocean) slave trade. During that time, traders from western Europe arrived in what is now **Senegal, Gambia, Guinea-Bissau, Mali, Angola, Congo, the Democratic Republic of Congo, Gabon, Nigeria, the Ivory Coast, Ghana, Sudan, and the Cameroon.** They traded their goods for human beings who were sold into slavery in the Caribbean, Brazil, and the United States. At least twelve million Africans were kidnapped and sold.

The African Diaspora also refers to people from African countries who settle in different parts of the world today.

E is for Explore, Education

Education has always been an important part of our story. Most enslaved people were not allowed to read or write. By making literacy illegal, their enslavers controlled the information they had access to and prevented them from sending messages to one another. Or so the enslavers thought. Many enslaved people found a way, often at great risk.

After Emancipation, many formerly enslaved people saw education as a path to true freedom and equality. They went to Black-only schools, and in 1896, the Supreme Court made separate schools for Black children and white children the law. Fifty-five years later, in 1951, the parents of **Linda Brown (1943–2018)** wanted her to attend her neighborhood public school, which was only seven blocks away. But the school was for white children only, and Linda was Black. The nearest school for Black children was twenty-one blocks away. Encouraged by the National Asso ciation for the Advancement of Colored People (NAACP), Linda's parents sued the Topeka board of education. The case went all the way to the Supreme Court and was argued by **Thurgood Marshall (1908–1993)**, who would become the first Black justice on the Supreme Court. In 1954, the Court decided that there should not be separate public schools for Black children and white children anywhere in the United States. This was a good thing, but it also meant that many all-Black schools closed and thousands of talented Black teachers were suddenly out of work.

In 1957, nine students—**Minnijean Brown (1941–), Elizabeth Eckford (1941–), Ernest Green (1941–), Thelma Mothershed (1940–), Melba Pattillo (1941–), Gloria Ray (1942–), Terrence Roberts (1941–), Jefferson Thomas (1942–2010), and Carlotta Walls (1942–)**— tried to go to all-white **Little Rock Central High School** in Little Rock, Arkansas, but the governor and angry mobs blocked them for months. In 1960, when six-year-old **Ruby Bridges (1954–)** tried to go to an all-white school in New Orleans, the National Guard had to protect her from the angry crowd. Eventually, Ruby Bridges and the Little Rock Nine were allowed to go to school. Along with Linda Brown, they were among the first Black students to integrate all-white schools.

And who are **Matthew Henson (1866–1955)** and **Mae Jemison (1956–)**? Matthew Henson is the first Black person to reach the North Pole, as part of an expedition led by Robert Peary in 1909. Depending on your perspective, the North Pole is the top of the world, but Mae Jemison went even farther than that. On September 12, 1992, she became the first Black woman in space, as an astronaut aboard the space shuttle *Endeavor*.

F is for Food, Farm, Fried Fish, Folklore

Black people have been farming in the United States for four centuries, beginning with the forced labor of the enslaved. After the **Emancipation Proclamation** declared slavery illegal in the South in 1863, many African-Americans stayed on their enslavers' plantations and worked as **sharecroppers.** They rented the land they lived on, and they paid their rent with a portion of their crops. By 1920, there were nearly one million African-American farmers in the United States.

Soul food describes a style of African-American cooking that has its roots in the early farming and food preparation methods of the enslaved. Enslaved Africans were given small amounts of food weekly—often cornmeal, flour, lard, molasses, and leftover scraps of meat (including pig intestines, feet, and tails; ox tails; and chicken necks)—that they cooked and flavored as best they could. For fresh food, enslaved people hunted, fished, gathered nuts and berries, and grew vegetables for themselves. Some common soul food dishes include fried fish, ham hocks (pig knuckles), buttermilk corn bread, and mustard greens.

Enslaved people were not allowed to legally marry. Instead, at the end of a wedding ceremony, a couple would jump over a broomstick. This ceremonial practice of "**jumping the broom**" became the way that enslaved people could publicly commit to one another. Some African-Americans continue the practice today to honor their ancestors.

G is for Great Migration

Even though the Emancipation Proclamation ended slavery legally, African-Americans were not free in the South. Southern states created laws called Black Codes that restricted the movement and opportunities of the formerly enslaved. Black people were also terrorized and killed just for being Black, especially if they dared to fight back against the restrictive laws. And so, between 1915 and 1970, roughly six million Black people fled the South for better lives in the North, Midwest, and West. This was known as the **Great Migration** (to migrate means to move from one place to another). They traveled mostly by train to cities like Chicago, which became a home of blues music; New York, which became home to the Harlem Renaissance; and Detroit and Philadelphia, which also became centers of Black music and culture.

H is for Harlem, Heart, Langston Hughes, Zora Neale Hurston

Harlem, New York, has long been a center of Black creativity. In the 1920s, **W. E. B. Du Bois (1868-1963)** and intellectual powerhouse **Alain Locke (1885-1954)** believed it was time for a "new Negro," who excelled in literature and the arts. This was the beginning of an incredible period of Black excellence known as the **Harlem Renaissance** (renaissance means rebirth). Writers like **Langston Hughes (1902-1967), Zora Neale Hurston (1891-1960), James Weldon Johnson (1871-1938), Jean Toomer (1894-1967), Arna Bontemps (1902-1973), Countee Cullen (1903-1946),** and **Claude McKay (1889-1948)** created poetry and prose.

Performers like **Duke Ellington (1899-1974), Bessie Smith (1894-1937), Louis Armstrong (1901-1971), Ethel Waters (1896-1977), Bill "Bojangles" Robinson (1878-1949), "Ma" Rainey (1886-1939),** and **Eubie Blake (1887-1983)** lit up Harlem stages like the **Apollo Theater.** Thinkers like **Paul Robeson (1898-1976), Marcus Garvey (1887-1940),** and **Arthur Schomburg (1874-1938)** talked about freedom. Artists like **Henry O. Tanner (1859-1937), James Van Der Zee (1886-1983), Aaron Douglas (1899-1979),** and **Augusta Savage (1892-1962)** captured Black life on film, in paint, and in clay. There were opportunities for entrepreneurs, too, like **Lillian Harris Dean (1870-1929),** better known as **Pig Foot Mary,** who sold steamed pigs' feet from a baby carriage to hungry customers streaming out of late-night clubs.

Even though the Renaissance faded in the 1930s, Harlem remains an important center of African-American culture to this day.

I is for Imagine, Invent, Innovative

African-Americans have invented and elevated so many things! These are just a few.

George Washington Carver (ca. 1864-1943) was a scientist. He was in charge of the farming program at Tuskegee Institute, an all-Black college led by Booker T. Washington (1856-1915). Carver invented more than 300 peanut products (but not peanut butter).

Madam C.J. Walker (real name: Sarah Breedlove, 1867-1919) cared for our hair. Her hair products and New York salon made her the first self-made woman millionaire in the United States.

Gwendolyn Brooks (1917-2000) was a poet. She often wrote about Bronzeville, her Chicago neighborhood, and became the first Black poet laureate of the United States.

Alvin Ailey (1931-1989) danced. He founded a modern dance troupe that performed dances celebrating Black culture. The Alvin Ailey American Dance Theater is still around today.

DJ Kool Herc (1955–) helped invent hip-hop. He extended the drum break of every song so people could find their groove. If you ever hear anyone say, "These are the breaks!" or "Break it down!" thank DJ Kool Herc.

Jean-Michel Basquiat (1960–1988) made art. He made art all over New York City that was unlike anything anyone had ever seen. Jean-Michel Basquiat had a voice.

J is for Juneteenth, J'ouvert Morning

On June 19, 1865, Union troops marched into Texas—the last state where people were still enslaved—and announced that the Civil War was over and all enslaved people were free. The date, June 19th, became known as **Juneteenth.**

J'ouvert means "morning" or "break of day" in French. Today, in Caribbean countries like Trinidad, Tobago, Grenada, and anywhere there is a large Caribbean population, J'ouvert is part of Carnival, a joyful celebration before the quieter period of prayer and fasting known as Lent.

J'ouvert started in Trinidad. In the early 1800s, the British brought 700 enslaved people from America to settle in Trinidad. There were also French landowners living in the area, and to mark the harvest, they held celebrations called *Canboulay.* In 1838, when slavery in Trinidad was abolished, the newly freed people took over the *Canboulay* celebrations and made them their own, adding dance and music traditions that had been forbidden while they were enslaved. Over time, these celebrations became what we now know as J'ouvert.

K is for Kin, Kwanzaa

Kwanzaa is a seven-day celebration that was created in 1966 by **Dr. Maulana Karenga (1941–)** to celebrate family and community. Kwanzaa is celebrated from December 26 to January 1 every year, and each day has a meaning:

Day 1: **Umoja** (unity)

Day 2: **Kujichagulia** (self-determination, or believing in your own strength)

Day 3: **Ujima** (collective work and responsibility, or taking care of our kin)

Day 4: **Ujamaa** (cooperative economics, or working hard to create new businesses and support other businesses in the community)

Day 5: **Nia** (purpose)

Day 6: **Kuumba** (creativity)

Day 7: **Imani** (faith)

The seven principles are represented each day by lighting a candle held in a *kinara.* The language of Kwanzaa is Kiswahili, which is spoken in many African countries and is the official language of Tanzania and Kenya.

L is for Love

Rose and Ashley (mid-1800s) were mother and daughter. Both were enslaved. When Ashley was sold at the age of nine, Rose hardly had time to say goodbye. She gave Ashley a sack that held the scraps of a dress, handfuls of pecans, and a braid of Rose's hair. They never saw each other again, but the sack has survived generations.

Nat Love (1854–1921) was a cowboy. He herded cattle in Texas and Arizona before giving up that life to work on the railroad.

Ruby Dee (1922–2014) and **Ossie Davis (1917–2005)** were love. This pioneering power couple acted in plays (in the original production of *A Raisin in the Sun*, for example) and movies, and they fought for humanity and freedom everywhere.

Mildred Loving (1939–2008) loved. She married a white man even though it was illegal for Black and white people to be married in her home state of Virginia. Her case went all the way to the Supreme Court, which decided that her marriage was legal and true.

Marsha "Pay No Mind" Johnson (1945–1992) was a transgender activist. She demanded to be recognized as her full self and fought for gay, lesbian, transgender, and bisexual people to be fully recognized, too.

M is for March, Matter

Marches—taking to the street in large, peaceful protests—send a powerful message. One of the best-known marches is the 1963 **March on Washington for Jobs and Freedom.** Two hundred and fifty thousand people gathered in Washington, D.C., to hear Dr. Martin Luther King, Jr. deliver his "I Have a Dream" speech. In it, he outlined his vision of a unified America. But the March on Washington wasn't the only march of the civil rights movement. There were smaller marches and boycotts in cities across the nation calling for better jobs, better housing, and better lives.

On March 7, 1965, **John Lewis (1940–2020)**, who believed in making "good trouble," and would later become a US congressman, attempted to lead a march from Selma, Alabama, to Montgomery, the state capital. He and his followers wanted the government to lift the restrictions that prevented Black people from voting. State troopers and local police brought the march to a violent end, and the event became known as **Bloody Sunday.** Finally, on March 21, 3,200 people marched out of Selma. Five days, fifty-four miles later, and 25,000 people strong, the marchers arrived in Montgomery.

In 2012, seventeen-year-old **Trayvon Martin (1995–2012)**, who was Black, was shot and killed. A year later, when the man who killed Trayvon was not found guilty of murder, **Patrisse Khan-Cullors (1984–)**, **Alicia Garza (1981–)**, and **Opal Tometi (1984–)** started an organization called Black Lives Matter to protect and uplift Black people. In 2020, after **Ahmaud Arbery (1994–2020)**, **Breonna Taylor (1993–2020)**, and **George Floyd (1973–2020)** were senselessly killed, "Black Lives Matter" was the rallying cry at protests around the world.

N is for Newspapers

The rich tradition of African-American newspapers and periodicals began as a way to further the cause of the abolitionist (anti-slavery) movement. *The North Star* was an antislavery newspaper founded by the abolitionist **Frederick Douglass (1818–1895)** in 1847.

African-American newspapers are a source of information, political activism, and pride for the Black community. Some of these major newspapers include the *Chicago Defender, Pittsburgh Courier, Richmond Planet,* and *Chicago Bee.*

Ida B. Wells (1862–1931) was a newspaper journalist. Beginning in the 1890s, she shed light on the many violent deaths of African-Americans at the hands of white people in the South. These murders are called lynchings. Wells researched her articles carefully and published them in a newspaper she co-owned called *The Memphis Free Speech and Headlight,* among others. Wells's writing was so widely read that she was sometimes known as the "princess of the press."

From newspapers to glossy magazines . . . **Johnson Publishing Company** was founded by **John H. Johnson (1918–2005)** in 1942 and was, at one time, the largest Black-owned publishing company in the world. Johnson Publishing Company published the *Negro Digest, Jet,* and *Ebony* magazine, which is still in print today.

O is for Organize, Organizations

Protests, boycotts, and marches all need someone to pull them together. Here are some of the major African-American organizations and organizers.

Student Nonviolent Coordinating Committee (SNCC): SNCC was founded in 1960 to give a voice to young people and students in the civil rights movement.

Congress of Racial Equality (CORE): CORE was founded in 1942 and worked with other civil rights groups to launch the **Freedom Summer** voter registration project, the **Freedom Rides** (aimed at desegregating buses and bus terminals), and the March on Washington for Jobs and Freedom in 1963.

Diane Nash (1938–) is a civil rights leader who began as a student activist in SNCC. She participated in the Freedom

Rides and helped to integrate lunch counters and bus terminals. She continues to fight for a fairer world.

Fred Hampton (1948–1969) was an activist and revolutionary. He was a leader in the **Black Panther Party** in Chicago and founded the Rainbow Coalition, a multicultural alliance that worked toward social change.

Ella Baker (1903–1986) was a leading activist and organizer in the civil rights movement. She worked with the NAACP and helped to found Martin Luther King, Jr.'s Southern Christian Leadership Conference and SNCC.

Bayard Rustin (1912–1987) helped Dr. King understand the power of breaking unjust laws and was a key organizer of the March on Washington. He was criticized for being gay but remained true to who he was.

P is for Power, Black Panthers, People, President

In many ways, the struggle of African-Americans has always been about power: A fight against the powers that hold us back, and a fight for the power that comes with being truly free.

In the 1960s and 1970s, "**Black Power**" was a rallying cry. It was first used publicly by **Stokely Carmichael** (later named **Kwame Ture, 1941–1998**) in 1966. "Black Power" was a call for African-Americans to come together, rise up, and take back the rights and freedoms they had long been denied. There are many different kinds of power. Here are a few people and groups who wielded it in their own ways:

The Black Panther Party was a political group formed by **Bobby Seale (1936–)** and **Huey P. Newton (1942–1989)** in Oakland, California, in 1966. The Black Panthers sought to protect African-American neighborhoods from police brutality and to help feed African-American children.

In fact, the school breakfast and lunch programs that exist in some schools today were inspired by the work of the Black Panthers.

Shirley Chisholm (1924–2005) was the first Black woman in Congress, where she proposed laws that gave more power to women and African-Americans. In 1972, she became the first woman and the first African-American to seek the nomination of a major party in a presidential election. And when she wrote the story of her life, she called it *Unbought and Unbossed.*

Barack Obama (1961–) was the 44th president of the United States and the first African-American to serve in that office.

In 2020, California senator **Kamala Harris (1964–)** became the first Black woman to be nominated for vice president (or president) by a major political party. Harris is an attorney, and the second Black woman ever to serve in the Senate. (The first was **Carol Moseley Braun (1947–)** of Illinois.)

Q is for Queens

There are ancient queens, queens who were heroes in our history, and queens who live among us today. Their royalty comes from their accomplishments and power. Not all queens wear crowns.

Queen Nefertiti (1370 BCE–1330 BCE) was an ancient Egyptian queen renowned for her beauty. She ruled alongside Pharaoh Akhenaten and was perhaps one of the most powerful women who has ever ruled.

Queen Amina (mid-sixteenth century) was queen of a medieval African kingdom called Zazzou, in present-day Nigeria. She was also a skilled warrior and a legend among the Hausa people.

Queen Nandi Ndlovukazi kaBhebe (1766–1827) of what is now South Africa, was queen mother of the Zulus and the daughter of Bhebhe, a past chief of the Langeni tribe. She was a mother who fought hard to protect herself and her children. Her son Shaka became a famous Zulu king.

Queen Yaa Asantewaa (mid-1800s–1921) was an Ashanti queen from present-day Ghana who inspired her people to fight for independence against British rule.

Ruby Hurley (1909–1980) was known as the "Queen of Civil Rights" and was a leader in the civil rights movement and within the NAACP.

Leontyne Price (1927–) is an American opera singer who is known around the world for her voice. She made her debut at the Metropolitan Opera on January 27, 1961.

Toni Morrison (1931–2019) was one of America's greatest authors. She was also a book editor, college professor, and mother.

Angela Y. Davis (1944–) is an activist, feminist, revolutionary, and scholar. Today, she focuses much of her power on changing the prison system.

Michelle Obama (1964–) is a lawyer, an author, and a former first lady of the United States (she is married to America's 44th president, Barack Obama). She is the closest thing we have to American royalty.

R is for Rise, Reach, Relentless, Refuse

Here are just a few African-American athletes you should know. Go, team!

Jesse Owens (1913–1980) was a runner. At the 1936 Olympics (held in Germany at a time when German leader Adolph Hitler had declared that white people were superior to everyone else), Owens won four gold medals for track and field events.

Jackie Robinson (1919–1972) rose out of the Negro Leagues to become the first African-American baseball player to play in the majors. He faced a lot of discrimination along the way and was ultimately the first Black player inducted into the Baseball Hall of Fame.

Althea Gibson (1927–2003) was a champion. She was a tennis and golf superstar.

Muhammad Ali (1942–2016) was a championship boxer and political activist. He fought for civil rights and rose up against war.

Arthur Ashe (1943–1993) was an American tennis player who accomplished many firsts. He was the first, and remains the only, African-American man to be ranked the number one tennis player in the world.

Florence Griffith Joyner (1959–1998) had style. Also known as Flo-Jo, she was the fastest woman in the world. And she had the most amazing long fingernails.

Shani Davis (1982–) is fast. He grew up on roller skates and became one of the fastest speed skaters in the world.

Gabby Douglas (1995–) is an Olympic gymnast and the first African-American to win the individual all-around event.

S is for Scientists, Stars, Study, Soul, Sweet, Sound, Sang

Benjamin Banneker (1731–1806) was a free Black man during the time of slavery and a self-educated scientist, farmer, almanac writer, and mathematician.

Dr. Daniel Hale Williams (1858–1931) was a doctor and the first person to open a hospital with an integrated staff. He was one of the first doctors to perform open-heart surgery.

Charles Henry Turner (1867–1923) was a zoologist who made many discoveries that have helped us learn more about the natural world. He was especially interested in the habits of honeybees.

Vivien Thomas (1910–1985) was an African-American laboratory supervisor who, even without a medical degree, discovered a way to save babies with a dangerous heart condition.

Katherine Johnson (1918–2020) was an African-American mathematician and author. She made important contributions to the US space program and helped astronauts go to the moon.

Dr. Patricia Bath (1942–2019) was the first African-American ophthalmologist and an inventor. She developed new ways to help people see more clearly and accomplished many firsts in her field.

Kizzmekia Corbett (1986–) is a scientist who studied the novel coronavirus that caused the 2020 pandemic.

She led a team that was first in the world to test a possible vaccine.

What is soul? There's no one answer to that question, except that it has its roots in the music and feeling of the African-American church. Here are a few of the most soulful people we know:

Sister Rosetta Tharpe (1915-1973) grew up singing in church before she became the Godmother of Rock 'n' Roll.

Ray Charles (1930-2004) is known as the High Priest and the Genius of Soul.

James Brown (1933-2006) is known as the Godfather of Soul.

Aretha Franklin (1942-2018) is known as the Queen of Soul, and **Sam Cooke (1931-1964)** as the King.

T is for Tuskegee Institute, Trade, Toil, Tools, True

The Tuskegee Institute was founded in 1881 by Booker T. Washington and was one of the first of higher learning for African-Americans. Tuskegee Institute was also the training ground for the US military's first 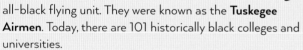 all-black flying unit. They were known as the **Tuskegee Airmen**. Today, there are 101 historically black colleges and universities.

Booker T. Washington (1856-1915) was a thinker, educator, and author. At one time, he was the most famous African-American in the country! He believed that farming and hard labor were the best ways for Black people to gain the respect of white society.

W. E. B. Du Bois, on the other hand, wasn't as concerned about respect. He thought Black people should demand better, and that talented intellectuals should lead the fight. In 1909, he helped found the NAACP.

U is for United States

When the US Constitution was first written in 1787, its opening line, "We the people," did not include African-Americans. In fact, Black people were not fully counted as people at all. The white men who wrote the Constitution thought that the amount of money and recognition each state got from the federal government should be based on the number of people living in that state. Trouble was, more people lived in the northern states than in the South. But there were far more enslaved people in the South than in the North. To balance things out, the authors debated our humanity. They decided that each enslaved African should count as three-fifths of a person. According to Federalist Paper No. 54, which explains the authors' thinking, enslaved people could not be considered fully human *because they were not free.*

The **13th Amendment** of the Constitution **(1865)** abolished slavery except as a punishment for a crime. The **14th Amendment (1868)** granted the formerly enslaved American citizenship, and the **15th Amendment (1870)** granted Black men—but not women—the right to vote (though, as seen above, those rights were in question well into the 1960s).

Harriet Tubman (ca. 1820-1913) was an enslaved woman who liberated herself and freed hundreds of others. Tubman was also a conductor in the **Underground Railroad,** a network of safe houses where the enslaved hid as they escaped. When the states went to war over the issue of slavery, Harriet Tubman spied for the Northern army.

And that flag? It's inspired by the work of artist **David Hammons (1943-)**, who in 1990 created a piece called *African-American Flag.* The colors have been used to represent African-American culture since Marcus Garvey used them in the Black Liberation flag: Red stands for the blood shed in the fight for freedom. Black stands for Black people, and green stands for growth.

V is for Vote

A vote is one of the most powerful forces for change, and Black people have fought for that power for centuries. One of the earliest voices in this fight was **Sojourner Truth (1797–1883)**. Born Isabella Baumfree, she also fought for women's rights and the end of slavery. One of the most visible fighters in later years was **Fannie Lou Hamer (1917–1977)**. In 1964, she helped organize Freedom Summer, an effort to register Black voters in Mississippi.

In 1965, after John Lewis marched from Selma to Montgomery, Alabama, President Lyndon B. Johnson signed the Voting Rights Act. It was meant to protect Black voters, especially in the South where they were often threatened or prevented from voting in other aggressive ways. In 2013, the Supreme Court removed some of these protections. In 2019, the House of Representatives, led by John Lewis, voted to put them back in. The issue has not been resolved, and the fight to vote freely continues.

W is for Writers, Wisdom, Words

There's a long tradition of African and African-American storytelling from folktales to rap. **Arthur Schomburg (1874–1938)** was a writer and collector of Black history. In 1911, in Harlem, he cofounded the Negro Society for Historical Research to celebrate work by Black authors. He collected books and manuscripts from all over the world, which eventually became part of the New York Public Library's collection. Today, the Schomburg Center for Research and Black Culture—part of the New York Public Library system—sits on Malcolm X Boulevard in Harlem.

X is for Malcolm X

Malcolm X (1925–1965), born Malcolm Little, was a political leader, speaker, and father. He went to prison as a young man, where he studied Islam and became a Muslim. He also changed his name from Malcolm Little to Malcolm X, rejecting the last name he believed tied him to slavery. (Enslaved people were given the last name of their enslavers to show ownership.)

When he was released from prison, X became a key player in the fight for civil rights. He believed in using any means necessary to advance the cause. However, after visiting the city of Mecca in Saudi Arabia (the holiest city in the Islamic faith) and seeing Muslims of all backgrounds come together, he embraced a more peaceful path. He also changed his name to El-Hajj Malik El-Shabazz.

Y is for Young, Gifted and Black, You

Lorraine Hansberry (1930–1965) was a playwright in Chicago. Her best-known work, *A Raisin in the Sun,* tells the story of life in a kitchenette apartment on Chicago's south side. Kitchenettes were tiny rooms that many Black families were forced to crowd into because of unfair housing laws in the city. Hansberry borrowed the name of her play from a poem by Langston Hughes. After Hansberry's death, a friend shaped the writings she left behind into a play about her life, called *To Be Young, Gifted and Black.* Another good friend, Nina Simone, borrowed the title for a song.

Nina Simone (1933–2003) was a singer, songwriter, and activist. Her song **"To Be Young, Gifted and Black"** became an anthem of the civil rights movement in 1969.

Z is for Zenith

Zenith means peak, like the top of a mountain. It is also the time when something is at its most powerful.

On April 3, 1968, Martin Luther King, Jr. delivered what has become known as his "Mountaintop Speech." In it, he said:

"We've got some difficult days ahead. But it doesn't matter with me now. Because I've been to the mountaintop . . . And I've looked over. And I've seen the Promised Land. I may not get there with you. But I want you to know tonight, that we, as a people, will get to the promised land!"

The next day, Dr. King was killed.

And when he fell, it was someone else's turn to push forward, just as Dr. King took his turn from those who came before.

And so we'll march on, 'til victory is won.